Rag to Richest with E-Bay

E-BAY made me Wealth 2014 !!!!

Dayshawn Thorpe

Copyright © 2014 Dayshawn Thorpe

All rights reserved.

ISBN-13: 978-1502922373
SBN-10: 1502922371

DEDICATION

To all the dreamers that don't know the words can't, i quit I give up !!!!

Just remember a goal is a dream with a deadline so keep on moving.

CONTENTS

	Acknowledgments	i
1	Buy and Sell item on Ebay	Pg #1
2	SELLING OTHERS PEOPLES ITEMS ON E-BAY	Pg #11
3	HOW TO SET UP A CONSIGNMENT BUSINESS ON E-BAY	Pg #13
4	DROP-SHIPPER'S	Pg #15
5	Researching E-Bay Bidders to Win an Auction	Pg #18
6	WHY ADD PAYPAL	Pg #20
7	SETTING UP YOUR PAYPAL	Pg #22
8	SETTING UP YOUR PAYPAL ON E-BAY	Pg #27
9	SELLING YOUR TALENT EBAY	Pg #29
10	I SOLD MY STUFF ON E-BAY	Pg #32

ACKNOWLEDGMENTS

You know how it is. You pick up a book, flip to the dedication, and find that, once again, the author has dedicated a book to someone else and not to you. Not this time.

THIS IS FOR YOU

CHAPTER 1

BUYING AND SELLING ITEMS ON EBAY

This guide is meant for the person just starting out on E Bay. I have been buying and selling on EBay for several years. I know the following tips would have saved me a lot of hassles and made me more money.

1. **Invest in a digital camera.** Having pictures of the items you sell (And not using stock photos from the manufacturer's web site) will put your bidders at ease. If they can see it they will be more apt to bid up on it and buy it. I am not saying for you to run out and get the most expensive digital camera you can buy. For $80-$100 you can get a good camera that will do the job just fine. Once you get your camera experiment with it. Take pictures of everyday items with different light sources (Sunlight, flash, desk lamp etc.) Basically get used to it before you post grainy, out of focus pictures on eBay.

2. **Don't sell the big dollar items right away.** If you have a Mickey Mantle rookie card you are dying to sell on eBay don't make that your first item. Build up your positive feedbacks. People are a little shy about putting down thousands of dollars on an item with someone who has 3 positive feedbacks.

3. **Buy and sell as many little things as you can.** This has to do with #2. Sell any of that

garage sale stuff you have lying around the house or buy some small stuff (Like a screwdriver set, a DVD, packing tape etc) These transactions will build up your feedbacks (And bidder's confidence)

4. **Do some research.** After you have gotten your feedbacks into the double digits you can start selling the bigger items. Do a search of your item on eBay. See what keyword other's are using to sell the same item. See if there is a market for your Widget. Save the item in your My eBay to find out what the final prices are. This will save you time and money. You don't want to put up your Limited Edition Signed Widget if there are 500 listed with no bids. Chances are you are going to be out the listing fee.

5. **DONT'S.** Don't say in your description: "Boyfriend's/girlfriend's/mother's/father's Widget I inherited/found in attic/garage/basement/Aunt Edna's house (etc., etc.,)..." Even if it is true there are a million people saying it on eBay. It sounds made up. Don't sell your item for 25 cents and charge $40 Shipping and Handling. This will sour new people you catch in this trap on eBay. Don't EVER click on the Respond Now button in an email. Even if it is from eBay, you can log on to My eBay and go to Messages and respond from there. Close all browser windows and restart your browser. Type in eBay.com in the address area. This will insure you are actually going to eBay and not a fake site. Fake or 'Phishing' emails look exactly like emails from eBay. If you enter

your info in these fake links they will be used to hijack your account.

6. **Make sure you have the item.** This may be a no brainer but make sure you have the item in your possession before you sell it. Don't post an item for $50 that you saw in a shop for $1. Don't let Uncle Bubba talk you into selling the vase he knows he has in his basement somewhere. Trying to explain to a buyer that the item you sold them is "out of stock" is not a good way to run a business.

7. **Shipping and Handling.** Make sure you know how much an item is going to cost to PACK and SHIP. Know what the box is going to cost and how much all of it together is going to weigh so you know exactly what it is going to cost to get to the buyer. Go the extra mile and wrap it in bubble wrap, it will impress your buyer. Spend the extra money on delivery confirmation. I have never had anyone say they didn't get their package but on the other hand I use delivery confirmation. State in your description if you will send items to Canada, Alaska, Hawaii, Europe etc. These places are expensive to send items to. Canada can be really expensive (More then you would think) so be forewarned.

8. **Feedback.** Give as much information as possible in your feedback. Did the buyer pay as soon as the auction was over? Did the seller contact you right away? Did the seller use bubble wrap? Was the item exactly as described?

9. **Solving selling issues.** "A person's perception IS their reality". If a buyer contacts you about a problem with an item make sure they are specific. Why don't you like the item? Is it damaged? Did the description say it was red and the item showed up blue? These are the types of questions a seller needs to ask. If the buyer has a legitimate problem offer them a refund on Shipping and Handling first. If they say that is not enough you might have to have them return the item to you for a full refund. These are all judgment calls that you will have to make. Feel them out first with the S&H refund first. Communication is the key! Be polite and to the point in all correspondence. Don't accuse anybody of anything...ever. Make sure you respond to questions thru My eBay Messages (Assuming of course that the buyer sent an email question thru the eBay Ask Member a Question link.) This will insure eBay has copies of what is actually said in all emails. You never know when you will need to defend yourself.

10. **Know what you sell, sell what you know.** Your reputation is on every item you send out. Make sure it is something *you* would be happy with purchasing. "I bought 100 of these and just didn't look at them before I sent them out." won't fly with a buyer (or eBay, PayPal, etc.). I'll give an example: I purchased a DVD that was supposedly widescreen (As per the decription). When I got it the case and the

DVD inside said fullscreen. It was the fullscreen version. I emailed the seller and asked if there was a mix up and was wondering if I could get the widscreen. The seller got pissed and said "Obviously, I bought this off eBay and I was lied to first." She was nice enough to offer a $1 refund and the suggestion to rent the widescreen version from a video store and switch the video store copy for the one I bought from her. Nice. Check out the stuff you are selling before you sell it. Also, sell something you know and are familiar with. If you don't know anything about Barbie dolls don't start selling them on eBay.

11. **Be honest and specific.** Another no brainer but just a clarification. If an electronic item doesn't work say it! Don't say that you are not sure if it works. I sold a Craftsman drill in the case with a charger that didn't work. I stated that at the top of the description and at the bottom. It still sold for $35. If you know the "Autographed" picture of Babe Ruth is a re-print say it! Don't beat around the bush. I was at a nation wide pawn shop and was looking around. They had a 30 day money back guarantee on all items in the store. This was company policy. Then in the corner I came across a shelf of miscellaneous items (A DVD player, saw, drill etc.) There was a small sign on the shelf saying that these items were being sold "As is" (The ULTIMATE in red flag phrases for a buyer.) without a guarantee. Do you think these items actually worked all the time? A

lie by omission is still a lie.

12. **Get a PayPal account.** This is an absolute. This will alow you to buy and sell quickly on eBay. Make sure you register a credit card with PayPal and have a checking or savings account attached to your PayPal account. This allows instant payment from a seller or to a buyer and will speed up the entire process.

13. **Item description.** Try to pack as much information in your item description as you can think of. Answer any questions the buyer might have in the description. This will save you time on answering emails from buyers who have questions that could have been answered in the description. Is the item New in a shrink wrapped box? Is it damaged? Does it have any extras? These are the type of questions you will be kicking yourself for having to answer over and over again that could have been explained in the description. Try and post measurements. Like: The model Corvette is 13 inches long, 5 inches wide and stands 6 inches tall. Be specific and don't forget the small stuff. I'll give you an example: I sold an autographed Joe DiMaggio 8 x 10 picture. I said in the description several times it was real. I went out of my way to explain that Joe at one time had a pen in his hand and wrote his name down on this picture. He signed it. What I forgot to mention was that it was in a cheap plastic frame. I was so worried about people realizing it was a real signature that I forgot to put in the description that the frame was a

cheap plastic job. The buyer complained to me in an email (As I probably would have if our roles were reversed.) about the frame and I agreed and refunded his shipping charge. If I would have stated the frame was a cheap plastic one I would probably been OK.

14. **As a buyer, read the item description thoroughly.** Read all descriptions twice, including Shipping and Handling (S/H) charges and return policies. This will decrease the chance of "surprises" later on. For example there are sellers on eBay that will sell items for 99 cents and charge $20 for S/H. This is how many have figured out how to increase their profits by lowering insertion fees and final value fees since eBay does not charge sellers a percentage of S/H charges. In some cases you will pay more for S/H charges then the actual item and this is fine. For example I purchased a Firewire cable and PCI Card for my computer and camcorder. The item was under $2 but S/H was around $7. This is fine since the same type of item at a retail store goes for $20-$30. Another issue to look out for is some people selling their item considerably less then anyone else. Sometimes they are selling a used version of an item or a damaged item. Again, check the description. I was looking for Anti-Virus software for my computer. The one I was looking at was going for $70+ retail. On eBay the average was around $40 plus S/H. I found one guy selling it for $25 and FREE S/H. How was he able to do this?

Well, he wasn't actually selling the software on a CD in a box. He was selling the activation code. He had won it in some kind of promotion. The software could be downloaded from the manufacturer's web site. He emailed me the code (Thus the FREE S/H). Some people have the ability to sell things cheaper then others. Just look around.

15. **Buying thru an Auction or Buy It Now.** When searching auctions always place the search criteria in the Ending Soonest mode. This will allow you to gauge when an auction is going to end so you can bid on it at the end. A signed Babe Ruth bat at $100 with 5 days to go is NOT going to sell for $110. If you are looking for that special Widget and the first search results come up with an auction ending in an hour for $22 plus $5 S/H OR a Buy it Now for $24.95 plus $6 S/H, I would go with the Buy It Now. Why? Well the actual auction will probably go up in the next hour. Remember you still need to bid on the item and hope the guy with the bid below you won't out bid you. Also, I am a little impatient. I *know* I will get the Buy It Now item. I have a *chance* of getting the auction item. Basically don't bite at the first auction (Or Buy It Now for that matter) you see. Scroll down and look. Click on the Buy It Now tab at the top of the search results screen. This will only show Buy It Nows. Then you can place them in lowest to highest order (Since it doesn't matter when a Buy It Now ends). To this day it still blows my mind how many sellers do not follow Rule #4. I have

been looking for items and have clicked on the Buy it Now tab and sorted by Lowest Price plus S&H only to see very large price differences. One item I was looking for had a $55 difference between the lowest 3 or 4 sellers and the next half dozen or so sellers with THE EXACT SAME ITEM. $55! Really? Good luck with that.

16. **Make an Offer.** This is another feature as a seller you can place in your items. Be warned though because a buyer can only place three offers on any single item per 30 days. Where this can bite you back as a seller is the amount of the offer you can set to automatically accept. For example: I wanted to purchase an item that had a Buy it Now list price of $59.99. I made an offer of $45 which was instantly refused. Understandable. That is an almost $15 difference. But it started getting annoying when my bids of $50 and $55 were refused instantly also. If as a seller you KNOW you won't sell an item at a 10 percent discount fine, just don't waste the buyer's time by setting an unrealistic discount of less then $5. I didn't purchase the item from this seller because I felt my time was wasted in a useless haggling process from a seller who knew they weren't going to sell the item at more then a $5 discount.

CHAPTER 2

SELLING OTHERS PEOPLES ITEMS ON E-BAY

Lots of E-Bay sellers let you sell items on consignment, and several retail locations base their business on consignment sales. You take possession of the item from the owner and sell it on E-Bay. You're responsible for taking photos and marketing the auction on E-Bay — for a fee. In addition to the money you earn selling on consignment, you also get excellent experience for future auctions of your own merchandise.

E-Bay publishes a directory of consignment sellers that you can search by inserting your address. Check out who in your area is a registered Trading Assistant. Read their terms and fees. Consignment sellers charge varied amounts based on their geographic location (some areas can bear higher fees than others).

To set up your business for consignment sales, you should follow a few guidelines:

1. Design a consignment agreement (a contract) and send it to the owners of the merchandise before they send you their items.

    Doing so ensures that all policies are set up in advance and that no questions will arise after the transaction has begun.

2. Have the owners sign and send the

agreement to you (the consignor) along with the item.

3. Research the item based on past sales so that you can give the owners an estimated price range of what the item might sell for on E-Bay.

4. Photograph the item carefully and write a thoughtful selling description.

5. Handle all e-mail inquiries as though the item were your own; after all, your fee is generally based on a percentage of the final sale.

Many sellers charge a flat fee for photographing, listing, and shipping that ranges from $5 to $10 plus as much as a 30-percent commission on the final auction total (to absorb E-Bay fees). Other sellers base their fees solely on the final sale amount and charge on a sliding scale, beginning at 50 percent of the total sale, less E-Bay and payment service fees. You must decide how much you think you can make on an item.

CHAPTER 3

HOW TO SET UP A CONSIGNMENT BUSINESS ON E-BAY

Consignment sales are a popular way for you to help non-techie types by selling their items on E-Bay. Lots of sellers do it, and several retail locations base their business on it. Essentially you take possession of the item from the owner and sell it on E-Bay.

You're responsible for taking photos and marketing the auction on E-Bay — for a fee. In addition to the money you earn selling on consignment, you also get excellent experience for future auctions of your own merchandise

To set up your business for consignment sales, you should follow a few guidelines:

1. Design a consignment agreement (a binding contract), and send it to the owners of the merchandise before they send you their items.

    Doing so ensures that all policies are set up in advance and that no questions will arise after the transaction has begun.

2. Have the owners sign and give the agreement to you (the consignor) along with the item.

3. Research the item based on past sales so you can give the owners an estimated range of what the item might sell for on E-Bay.

4. Photograph the item carefully and write a thoughtful, thorough description.

5. Handle all e-mail inquiries as though the item were your own.

   After all, your fee is generally based on a percentage of the final sale.

Traditional auction houses handle consignment sales in a similar fashion.

CHAPTER 4

DROP-SHIPPER'S

A *drop-shipper* is a business that stocks merchandise and sells it to you (the reseller) — but ships the merchandise directly to your customer.

By using a drop-shipper, you transfer the risks of buying merchandise, shipping it, and storing it to another party. You become a stockless retailer with no inventory hanging around — often an economical, cost-effective way to do business.

The following steps outline the standard way to work with most drop-shippers via eBay:

1. Sign up on the drop-shipper's Web site to sell their merchandise on eBay or in your Web store.

Be sure you've checked out their terms before you sign up — to be sure there's no minimum purchase upon signing up.

2. Select the items from their inventory that you wish to sell.

For this example, say the item you select costs $6.99. The supplier gives you descriptive copy and photographs to help make your sales job easier.

3. Post the item online and wait (fidgeting with anticipation) for someone to buy it.

By the way, you'll be selling this item for $19.99 plus shipping.

4. As soon as your buyer pays for the item, e-mail the drop-shipper (or fill out a special secure form on their Web site) and pay for the item with your credit card or PayPal.

5. Relax while the drop-shipper ships the item to your customer for you.

6. If all goes well, the item arrives quickly and safely.

You make a profit and get some positive feedback.

The drop-shipper's Web site provides you with descriptions and images. Fine. But you and everybody else who sells that item on eBay will have the same photos and descriptive copy. Do yourself a favor and get a sample of your item, take your own pictures, and write your own description. Then at least you have a chance at beating the competitive "sameness" on eBay.

Drop-shipping works especially well for Web-based retail operations. Web stores can link directly to the drop-shipper to transmit shipping and payment information. When you're selling on eBay, it's another thing. There's more competition and you can't list hundreds of items at no additional cost.

Listing items on eBay costs money and may build up your expenses before you make a profit. You can't just select an item from a drop-shipper and throw hundreds of auctions on eBay without loosing money. That is, unless your item is selling like gangbusters at an enormous profit. If that were the case, you could count on meeting up with another eBay seller buying direct from the manufacturer and undercutting your price.

It's one thing to sign up for a free newsletter — or even to register with a particular site — but it's something else to have to pay to see what the drop-shipper intends to offer you. You should not pay anything in advance to sign up for a drop-shipping service.

Finding a good drop-shipper

Thousands of Web companies are aching to help you set up your online business. While some of them are good solid companies with legitimate backgrounds, others are out there just trying to get your money. These guys hope you don't know what you're doing; they're betting you'll be desperate enough to send them some cash to help you get your share of the (har-har) "millions to be made online."

Consider the following when you're choosing drop-shippers to work with:

- **Skepticism is healthy.** When you come across Web sites that proclaim that they can drop-ship thousands of different products for you, think twice. Thousands? How many stores carry "thousands" of items — if they do, they have vast square footage for storage and hundreds of thousands of dollars to invest in merchandise. Most drop-shipping services don't. A much smaller offering of merchandise may indicate that indeed the drop-shipper has the merchandise ready to ship and isn't relying on ordering it from someone for you.

- **Look out for long lines of distribution.** Drop-shippers are often middlemen who broker merchandise from several different sources — for example, from other middlemen who buy from brokers (who in turn buy from manufacturers). The line of distribution can get even longer — which means that a whole slew of people are making a profit from your item before you even buy it "wholesale." If even one other reseller gets the product directly from the distributor or (heaven forbid) the manufacturer, that competitor can easily beat your target selling price and make (what should have been) your profit. Verify with the drop-shipper that they stock the merchandise they sell.

Many wholesalers will perform drop-shipping for you.

When you find a drop-shipper who is also a wholesaler (or vise versa), look for one who has a good professional track record. Look for experienced buyers who get in a lot of good merchandise, and can handle pro-level business concerns such as resale permits and sales-tax numbers.

Coping with the inevitable "out-of-stock"

What happens when you sell an item and you go to the distributor's site and find it's sold out? Before your heart completely stops, call the drop-shipper. Perhaps they still have one or two of your items around their warehouse and took the item off the Web site because they're running too low on it to guarantee delivery.

If that isn't the case, you're going to have to contact your buyer and 'fess up that the item is currently out of stock at your supplier. Call your customers in this situation; they may not be as angry as they might if you just e-mailed them. Offer to refund their money immediately. Somebody else's foul-up may net you bad feedback, but that risk goes along with using drop-shipping as a business practice.

CHAPTER 5

Researching E-Bay Bidders to Win an Auction

To find the best price for any item on eBay, you need to research the item to find out what similar items on eBay tend to sell for. But eBay shows you more than just the winning bid; you can gain some insight into your competition by checking out previous auctions.

When you conduct your eBay research, the best strategy is to look at the prices achieved in previous sales. Do a search for completed auctions. Then check an auction's bid history by clicking the Bid History link on the auction item page (the link appears next to the number of bids). You'll be presented with a screen like the one shown here. This will at least give you an idea of how many people are duking it out for the item, if not their actual IDs.

Bidder	Bid Amount	Bid Time
l***r (204)	US $811.01	Jun-29-08 15:47:11 PDT
e***t (94)	US $801.01	Jun-29-08 18:50:50 PDT
e***t (94)	US $751.01	Jun-29-08 18:48:54 PDT
l***r (204)	US $666.63	Jun-29-08 14:51:18 PDT
e***t (94)	US $351.01	Jun-29-08 14:47:12 PDT
l***r (204)	US $329.69	Jun-25-08 15:27:28 PDT
j***3 (16)	US $312.01	Jun-25-08 20:00:44 PDT
j***3 (16)	US $301.06	Jun-25-08 19:59:59 PDT
j***3 (16)	US $275.06	Jun-25-08 19:59:18 PDT
j***3 (16)	US $251.06	Jun-25-08 19:58:49 PDT
j***3 (16)	US $205.06	Jun-25-08 19:58:20 PDT
l***r (204)	US $151.69	Jun-24-08 18:40:30 PDT
o***a (38)	US $100.00	Jun-24-08 22:47:42 PDT
	US $50.00	Jun-23-08 17:55:55 PDT

Bidders: 4 Bids: 13 Time left: 2 hours 36 mins 51 secs

An item's bidding history.

Pay attention to the times when <u>bidders</u> are placing their bids, and you may find that the people bidding in the auction are creatures of habit — making their bids about once a day and at a particular time of day. They may be logging on before work, during lunch, or after work. Whatever their schedules, you have great info at your disposal in the event that a bidding war breaks out: Just bid after your competition traditionally logs out, and you increase your odds of winning the auction.

Early in an auction, there may not be much of a bidding history for an item, but that doesn't mean you can't still check out the dates and times a bidder places bids. You can also tell whether a bidder practices <u>sniping</u> if his or her bid is in the last few seconds of the auction. You may have a fight on your hands if the bidder uses sniping.

CHAPTER 6

HOW TO USED E-CHECKS

E-CHECKS are the digital counterpoints of the pieces of paper found in a checkbook. Buyers and sellers pay and get paid by eCheck in electronic transactions similar to tradtional banking.

When someone sends you an eCheck as payment, the funds won't be deposited into your account for three or four days (however long it takes for the eCheck to clear).

Buyers paying with eChecks

From the buyer's standpoint, sending an eCheck is advantageous; the funds are left in the buyer's bank account for a few extra days, earning interest, and no credit card debt is incurred. To send an eCheck, in response to an invoice or Money Request, you need to have a bank (checking or savings) account linked to your PayPal account. Here's how to use eCheck to pay for a purchase:

1. When you receive a request for money, click the Pay button to make a payment.

2. On the Pay Money Request page, click the More Funding Options link under the Funding Options section of the page.

3. On the Funding Options page, select the eCheck option and choose which bank account to use.

If necessary, you can link a new bank account to your PayPal account by clicking the Add Bank link.

4. Click the Continue button.

Verify the payment details and click the Send Money link.

Sellers receiving eChecks as payment

If you receive an eCheck payment, you get a PayPal e-mail informing you that "Cash is on the Way!" If you hoped for "Cash is Already Here!" you may feel a little disgruntled, but the good news is that you'll get payment in three or four days.

If you look at the transaction in your PayPal Account Overview, you see a status of Uncleared until the funds are transferred from the buyer's bank account. It's important that you don't mail any items to the buyer until after the payment has cleared.

CHAPTER 7

WHY ADD PAYPAL

If you think PayPal is just for eBay sales, then you're missing out on a great opportunity to get revenue (or more revenue) from your Web site. If you're not already selling products from your Web site, adding Buy Now buttons or the PayPal Shopping Cart is the easiest way to turn a marketing site into an e-commerce site. If you're already accepting credit card payments, then offering PayPal as an additional payment option widens your customer base because people who don't want to use a credit card can still make purchases.

PayPal is the easiest way to add e-commerce to your Web site

If you don't know how to code, but you're comfortable using FrontPage to create a Web site, you can integrate e-commerce quickly and easily with PayPal's free tools for Microsoft FrontPage. These tools let you add Buy Now buttons, a Shopping Cart, or set up subscriptions and recurring payments while you're designing with FrontPage.

You don't need to apply for a merchant license

In order to sell and accept credit cards online, you normally need to work with a credit card processing company or bank. The role of the processor is to validate buyer's credit cards at the time of purchase. Credit card processors help prevent you from fraud by checking whether the buyer's credit card is valid, and blocking IP addresses, e-mail addresses, or names of known problem buyers. Additionally, the processor can block a payment that sends the user over their credit limit.

You get a lot of peace of mind when working with a processor, but the application process can be a pain. (You need to provide a lot of information about your company, have a business bank account, and so on.) After the processing company approves you, you need to set up your Web site to accept secure payments and to configure your e-commerce software to send payment data to your processor's payment gateway. To work with a credit card processor, you spend a lot of time and resources before selling your first item.

PayPal also lets you accept secure payments, even credit card purchases, but the application process is as easy as providing your country, name, address, home telephone number, and e-mail address, and accepting the PayPal User Agreement. You can decide to open an e-commerce shop in the morning and start accepting payments in the afternoon.

You can specify payment preferences

If you accept PayPal payments, you can set up your Payment Receiving Preferences to block certain types of buyers. You can decide not to sell internationally or to block purchases from buyers who have not confirmed their address. This adds another layer of protection for you as the seller. Additionally, you can decide to accept payments only if they are made in a specific currency, and you can block buyers who try to purchase with a credit card when they have a bank account linked to their credit account.

In addition to deciding whether to block certain types of buyers, you can easily change your credit card company name (the one that is shown on the buyer's credit card statement).

The buttons are free

Most credit card companies charge you a monthly fee, even if you don't receive any payments. Adding PayPal e-commerce buttons to a Web site costs you nothing — if you don't sell anything, you don't pay. When you do sell an item, you pay $0.30 for each transaction, plus 2.9 percent of the selling price. The percentage can drop as low as 1.9 percent, depending upon your monthly volume of sales.

Easy encryption

When you want to set up a secure e-commerce Web site, there are a number of steps you must take. First, you need to apply for an SSL (Secure

Sockets Layer) license. SSL is a protocol used to send secure data over the Internet. SSL encrypts data that is sent from the browser; the data is decrypted when it gets to the server. After you implement SSL, you need to build an e-commerce Web site that works with SSL to transmit data securely (usually to a credit card processor).

Compare this to the ease of encrypting buttons with PayPal! When creating a button with the Button Factory, all you have to do is click the Yes option to have your button's code encrypted. When you copy the encrypted code to your Web site page, snooping eyes won't be able to see any personalized information by viewing the source code for the Web page.

Setting up subscription payments is easy

PayPal makes it easy to set up subscriptions and recurring payments and frees you from the hassle of sending out periodic invoices. When you set up your subscription, you can specify up to two trial periods (for example, the subscriber can be billed $0.00 for the first month, and $20 for every month after the trial period has ended). You can set your billing cycle to be days, weeks, months, or even years.

You have the option of setting up *recurring payments,* in which the buyer pays the specified amount every month, without end. You can also set up payment installments; for example, you can charge the buyer $20 for five installments to purchase a $100 product.

Finally, PayPal can generate unique username and

password combinations if you want to give buyers access to "members-only" content, stored in a special folder of your Web site.

No setup fees

Usually setting up an online store involves some type of setup fee — either you have to pay for the price of the e-commerce software, a setup fee if you're using an online service, or you have to pay a developer to write custom code. Not with PayPal. . . . You have no upfront fees to open an online store if you use the PayPal Buy Now buttons or the Paypal Shopping Cart. With PayPal, you don't pay a thing until you actually sell something!

Detailed transaction data

When you use PayPal for e-commerce transactions, you can use the PayPal History Reporting Tools to download and analyze detailed information about every sale made. You have the option of including Shopping Cart details in the report. You can also do an advanced search to find transactions linked to an e-mail address, transaction ID, buyer's name, receipt ID, or item number. You can import the downloaded file into Excel, Quicken, or Quick-books for additional tracking and analysis. You can also look at summary information available from the Merchant Sales Report.

Promotion through PayPal shops

If you accept PayPal payments on your Web site, you can enroll your online store in PayPal Shops, a directory of Web sites that accept PayPal. After you enroll, PayPal members can search for the products and services you sell.

There is no cost to list your site with PayPal Shops, but you do need to have a Premier or Business PayPal account. Additionally, you need a bank account and credit card linked to your PayPal account and you need to invest in the PayPal Money Market Fund. To enroll in the fund, you need to provide a social security number or an employer identification number.

CHAPTER 8

SETTING UP YOUR PAYPAL ON E-BAY

You start setting up your PayPal profile during the process of registering for a PayPal account. Open up your and browser type **www.paypal.com** into the Address Bar. The PayPal home page has multiple links that let you sign up for your free account. You can find one <u>Sign Up</u> link in the upper-right corner of the screen, and the other can be found in the middle of the screen.

Opening a Personal account

You can open a Personal account in just a few steps; the entire process doesn't usually take more than five minutes. Here's how:

1. At the PayPal Account Sign Up page, make sure the Personal Account option is selected.

If you're wondering what happened to the Premier account , just hang on. You have the option of upgrading a Personal account to a Premier account later on.

2. Select your country from the list and click the Continue button.

3. Start building a PayPal profile by filling in the fields shown on the Account Sign Up page.

The information you need to give PayPal includes

• Your first name, last name, and full address, including city, state, zip code, and country. PayPal requires a zip code for U.S. accounts, but may not require one if you create an International PayPal account.

• Your home telephone number for verification purposes; you have the option of entering a work number.

• Your e-mail address. You need to enter this twice so PayPal can ensure you didn't mistype it the first time.

• A password to use with your PayPal account.

• This password must be at least eight characters long and is case-sensitive. (This means you need to pay attention to whether you use uppercase and/or lowercase characters when you create your password. PayPal won't accept *PASSWORD123* as a valid password if you typed *password123* as your password when you created your account.) Just as you did when you entered your e-mail address, you need to type your password a second time. Picking a password that you don't use with other accounts you may have is also important. If you pick your e-mail password to use as your PayPal password and your e-mail password is compromised, you may find someone making unauthorized use of your funds! It's better to be safe and think up a unique password.

• You are asked to pick two questions from a list of four security questions. The answers you give to these questions are used to verify your identity if you lose or forget your password.

• Deciding whether you want to open a Personal or Premier account. The big advantage of having a Premier account is that you can accept credit card payments from people who don't have or use a PayPal account.

• You need to read and accept the PayPal User Agreement and Privacy Policy, or you won't be able to open your account. It's *vital* that you read both documents before checking the Yes option, indicating that you agree to the terms. Knowing what can or may happen to your account is important before transferring your money into the account.

• PayPal also asks you to indicate that you understand your rights with regard to the arbitration of claims as outlined in the Legal Disputes section of the User Agreement. A link is provided to the document, which describes how legal disputes should be handled in the event that there are problems between you and PayPal. As with any legal document, you should read the whole thing before signing and contact a lawyer if you're unsure as to what the document means.

• You have one final security step to go through before the account opens. PayPal displays a sequence of characters in a box with a boxed background. You must type in the characters, exactly as shown, in a text box to the right of the sequence. This step is to prevent automated programs from trying to sign up for PayPal accounts. Although a program can fill out the fields on the Account Sign Up page, it can't read the sequence and type it into the box.

• If you are visually impaired, you can still type the correct character sequence into the box, even if you can't read the characters as shown against the background. Click the Help link displayed at the end of the "Security Measure" paragraph to open the PayPal Registration Security Help page. At the end of the page is a listen to the security characters link. Click the link to hear an audio clip that says the characters aloud. You can then type the characters into the box correctly to finish the registration process. In the case of these security characters, it doesn't matter whether you type in the letters as uppercase or lowercase, as long as you get the letters and numbers in the correct sequence.

4. Click the Sign Up link at the bottom of the page to submit your registration information.

After filling out the registration form, you're taken to a page that tells you the process is almost complete except for the confirmation of your e-mail address. After you click the Sign Up link from the previous screen, PayPal sends you an e-mail.

5. Open your e-mail program and look for an e-mail from PayPal.

If your e-mail inbox is anything like mine, you have to search hard to find the PayPal e-mail amidst all the spam. Look for an e-mail from service@paypal.com with a subject heading of "Activate Your PayPal Account!"

6. Click the Click here to activate your account link, which can be found in the body of the e-mail. (Alternatively, you can copy the link and paste it into the address bar of your browser.)

Clicking the link takes you to a page where you are prompted to enter the password you designated when you registered for the account.

7. Type your password and click the Confirm button.

Congratulations! You just opened your PayPal account.

Updating your profile

After you open a PayPal account, keeping your user profile up-to-date is very important. To update your profile, log on to your account and click the Profile link under the My Account tab. You have the option of updating any of the following:

- **Account Information:** You can update your basic contact information (e-mail, address, password, time zone, and so on).

- **Financial Information:** You can change the

credit cards or bank accounts associated with your PayPal account, set up online bill paying, see your account balances, redeem gift certificates, and more. The options that are available are dependent upon the type of account that you have.

- **Selling Preferences:** Here you can set up preferences for setting up auctions, registering your Web site as a PayPal shop, setting shipping preferences, setting up invoice templates, and so on. The options available depend upon the type of PayPal account you have.

CHAPTER 9

SELLING YOUR TALENT ON EBAY

If you're talented in any way, you can sell your services on eBay. Home artisans, chefs, and even stay-at-home psychics are transacting business daily on the site. What a great way to make money on eBay — make your own product!

Many custom items do well on eBay. People go to trendy places (when they have the time) such as Soho, the Grove, or the Village to find unique custom jewelry. They also go to eBay. There's a demand for personalized invitations, cards, and announcements — and even return address labels. Calligraphic work or computer-designed items are in big demand today, but no one seems to have the time to make them. Savvy sellers with talent can fill this market niche.

CHAPTER 10
I SOLD MY STUFF ON E-BAY

When I say I sold my *stuff*, what I really mean is I sold my *crap.* Crap that I shouldn't have bought in the first place.

Earlier this year, I knew it was time to get rid of my remaining school loans once and for all. I've added two kids to the mix recently and judging by the estimates in cost of college, I'll be shelling out $100,000 per kid in 18 years even for state college tuition.

To add insult to injury, I'm not even using *either* of my two degrees in my daily life right now. Like I said, it's time to put these loans behind me!

The problem was how?

Our spending plan was already tight. I didn't want to tap into any of our savings. It certainty wasn't the type of *emergency* that dictated tapping the emergency fund. And the fees made withdrawing from our IRA and expensive option. On the income side, we already own 3 business and are raising 2 young kids, so getting another "j.o.b." or starting another side project seemed down right insane.

I had a burning desire to get these loans out of my life, but didn't now how it was going to happen.

But right after the holidays a bell went off in my head. As I began to look around our house and clean up after the post holiday madness, I realized how much *stuff* we owned. Bags, shoes, dvd's, books, ipods, old laptops, old kayaks, skis that didn't fit, bikes that we no longer used, the list went on for miles...

This was stuff we didn't love and certainly didn't need. So I started listing about 10 items a week on eBay (and a few larger items on Craigslist). Some weeks when I had a few extra hours I'd list more and other weeks I didn't have time to list anything.

I kept at it, though, and slowly but surely things started to sell. Every time my Paypal account reached $500 or $1000 I transferred it over to put an additional payment towards my student loan balance. Little by little the amount owed kept going down. When I got it under $10,000, I was stoked and motivated. Over the next few months, I saw it decrease to only $5,000, then $1,000, and then before I knew it... $0.

Since I've paid off the loan, though, I haven't stopped! I'm selling more stuff as we speak to pay for plane tickets to Mexico this winter.

Here come the excuses...

I hear them all the time...

- *"I don't have anything to sell."*

- *"No one wants my stuff."*

- *"I don't have time to learn how to sell stuff online."*

The truth is nearly everyone has stuff they can sell. It's much easier than you think and you'd be absolutely shocked at the prices people will pay for your neglected possessions!

ABOUT THE AUTHOR

Dayshawn Thorpe is a freelance writer, A how to e-book author. He writes for many online publications, as well as a Authors of two How to books. His latest project is a self help book on how to become wealthly using ebay compiling that will be published this year.

www.ingramcontent.com/pod-product-compliance
Lightning Source LLC
Chambersburg PA
CBHW070721180526
45167CB00004B/1562